WORKING OUT TOGETHER

Sharrel Keyes
Working Out Together
Keeping Your Group in Shape

Harold Shaw Publishers
Wheaton, Illinois

Cover photo: David Singer

ISBN 0-87788-263-0

Library of Congress Cataloging in Publication Data

Keyes, Sharrel.
　　Working out together.

　　Bibliography: p.
　　1. Bible—Study.　　2. Church group work.　　I. Title.
BS600.2.K49　1985　　　　220′.07　　　　84-23656
ISBN 0-87788-263-0

95　94　93　92　91　90　89　88　87　86　85

10　9　8　7　6　5　4　3　2　1

Contents

Acknowledgments

I would need hundreds of fingers and toes if I were to try to count the number of people who shared with me their love of God and the good news of God's love they've found in Scripture.

Some of the most special include those individuals who patiently listened to my endless questions and complaints when I was just discovering the Bible for myself; the men and women and college students with whom I have shared small group discussion studies over the past twenty years; the churches and organizations that gave me the opportunity to learn by teaching; the students who kept rattling my cage as they searched for more than superficial answers; cowriters, editors and publishers who believed along with me in the life-changing potential of Bible study; those who have prayed with me and for me and have shared the discipline of Scripture memory; and finally that whole bunch of mainly faceless (to me) people who've used our guides, started groups, and been challenged to renew their lives because of the Lord they've met in Scripture.

Won't it be great when we can all get together! Until then, thanks.

1

Goals for Your Bible Study Workout

SEVERAL YEARS AGO WHEN I WAS not only younger but brash enough to think I could do just about anything if I set my mind to it, I started leading a Bible study group. I wasn't approaching this task cold. I had been teaching a young adult Sunday school class and instructing groups of students and adults in personal Bible study and techniques for leading group discussions. So when I was asked to take over for a Bible study leader who was leaving town, I knew I was more than ready for the job.

That first week I probably broke every rule I had drummed into my students (and if I missed any, I made up for it the second week). I came on strong, my head full of lists on creating a successful group. My stomach was swarming with butterflies; it seemed as if the group's "success" depended on my demonstrating how good a leader I was.

I spent much of the first session imposing ground rules so that all members in the group would have an equal chance to share what they had discovered in the passage without fear of being "wrong." Then, within ten minutes, I was telling a shy, sensitive member of the group that she couldn't possibly believe what she had just said because it was doctrinally incorrect!

I obviously had a lot to learn about what happens in a good Bible study discussion and even more to learn about the kind of exercise it takes to keep a Bible study group "in shape."

As I've grown older, less green—and I hope a little wiser— I've learned some important lessons. I've learned that a theoretical knowledge of the correct facts and the "workout" techniques isn't enough; there is more required—a whole lot more. I needed time to get accustomed to those techniques so that I could relax more; I also needed to get more comfortable with myself; I needed to develop in social skills; and I needed to learn through experience how groups of people work together.

I've spent about twenty years learning that there's always more to learn. I'd like to give you a quick look at what I, and a whole lot of other people, have discovered about a very special activity—discussion Bible study. I hope that what we've experienced will help you and your group enjoy the process even more!

The fact that you're reading this book probably means that you and several friends are interested in discussing the Bible together. Perhaps you found that when you moved from "We'd like to . . ." to "Let's start . . ." you weren't sure how to put your interest into action.

You may have talked about what you want your group to be like and what you'd like to see happen as you meet together. I'd guess that the goals you've decided on are probably similar to guidelines other discussion groups have set. See how closely your list matches this one:

1/We've agreed to meet together regularly in order to discover what God is saying to us through his Word. The "regularly" is important to insure continuity. Ideas will carry over from week to week as themes develop in the Scripture we're studying. In order to accomplish this, we've made our study time a priority on our calendars, scheduling other activities around it.

As you make this kind of commitment to God and each other, he will be increasingly present to you individually and corporately, meeting you in Scripture and through the experiences and insights you share with each other. After all, it is his desire that you know him better and grow into the likeness of Christ.

2/We've agreed that all of us will seek to begin each study with a clean slate. No one will come with an established doctrinal position that must be defended at all costs. Rather, we will look at the text together, gaining fresh insight into the facts of the passage and the relationships between the ideas presented. In this way, we'll be able to see the main point in its context and then look for ways the passage affects our actions and beliefs.

This process, by the way, is the heart of the inductive method of Bible study and perhaps the most fruitful approach for group as well as personal study. A further explanation of this method will be given further on.

3/We've agreed to look for the growth points in our lives where the Bible can speak to us. We also give ourselves and each other freedom to ask questions of the text and of the group so that we can grow in understanding as we hold our own experiences and beliefs up to God's Word. We know that we can't "hurt" the Bible or God by asking questions, so we make the commitment to be honest, to voice doubts or hard questions rather than keeping silent or mouthing "right" (socially acceptable) answers. As we listen to and support each other, we will remember that what is shared remains the property of the group and will not be the subject of our next phone conversation.

As I encounter new experiences and directions in my own life, I discover that different passages or themes become important to me; or I find that I'm seeking answers for different sets of questions. Observing these changes within myself has helped me understand that my friends are also at varying places (intellectually, emotionally, and spiritually) in their relationships with God. I've found that I need to be sensitive to this variety and appreciate it rather than trying to force my neighbors to conform to my present pattern. As the group grows in trust and honesty, it will also grow in support and affirmation, and you will experience increasing freedom in sharing joys as well as questions.

4/We have agreed that no one in the group is the resident Bible expert. All of us are fellow students and the Holy Spirit speaking through God's Word is the teacher. Because the leader is not the authority, no one needs to feel inferior in knowledge or ability. In a real sense, we're all in this together.

For this study, your ability to read a common language and your willingness to ask honest questions of the text and of each other are more important tools than a seminary degree. Although the Christian community has a real need for pastors, teachers, and carefully written books—all of which can enlarge our understanding—none of them can substitute for this personalized learning in which individuals interact with God's Word, working in small, supportive groups to understand, share, and apply Scripture to present needs.

5/We have agreed to corporate ownership rather than passive membership in a teacher's class. Therefore, we will each accept a certain amount of responsibility so that the group can work together well. We will all contribute to the discussion and listen and respond to others' contributions and questions. We'll try not to get carried away with the point we want to make or the questions we want to ask; if they are significant, we won't forget them. We'll exercise some gentle discipline on ourselves and other group members in order to keep the discussion on track, curtail over-talkative members, and encourage silent observers to become participants.

The leader can use additional techniques to help the group work together well, but only after members understand that they are active participants in a creative, disciplined discussion. One of the ways to encourage the concept of group ownership is to pass around the role of discussion leader on a regular basis. Many groups find that rotating it weekly according to a prearranged schedule works best. When leadership is shared and the responsibility for a fruitful discussion rests equally on all shoulders, this book can serve as a helpful "refresher" for everyone. A copy should be given to any newcomers to your group.

6/We agree to undertake the discipline of prayer—specific, supportive, involved prayer—for each other during the week. We expect to see changes, the results of God working in the one praying and the one prayed for.

Praying for one another during the week can help establish and strengthen relationships as you share your hurts and needs and get to know each other on a deeper level.

2

What's So Great about the Inductive Method?

THE GOALS THAT WE'VE JUST LOOKED AT reflect the kind of group dynamics associated with the inductive approach. They support a central concept: that Bible study is highly effective when you discover for yourself what a passage says and decide what difference it will make in your life rather than being told what it means and what you should do about it.

How does the inductive study method work? Usually it deals with a single passage of Scripture for each study session and asks a series of questions which lead you through three levels:

1/*Observation*—learning what the passage says;

2/*Understanding*—discovering the relationship of ideas in the passage so you can grasp the main point;

3/*Application*—allowing the passage of Scripture to alter your thought patterns, emotional outlook, and/or behavior.

Let's look at an example from a studyguide to illustrate these types of questions. The passage for study is Genesis 41 which recounts Pharaoh's dreams, Joseph's interpretation of them, and Joseph's appointment as Pharaoh's second-in-command.

Take a moment to read through the Scripture passage before looking at the following questions.

1/How did both dreams emphasize the severity and certainty of the famine? In what way were Joseph's reactions to the dreams similar to those of Pharaoh and the rest of the court? In what ways did his reactions differ from theirs?

2/Why did Pharaoh believe Joseph? How did Pharaoh know his appointment of Joseph was justified?

3/What characteristics in Joseph allowed others to entrust him with responsibility?

4/What do you need to do now to become someone who can be given responsibility?

5/How did Pharaoh help Joseph do the job to which he appointed him?

6/What evidence is there from the chapter that Joseph's life was satisfying?

7/What ingredients does God provide to make your life whole?

8/How will you recognize your wholeness? (from *Genesis 26-50: Called by God* by Margaret Fromer & Sharrel Keyes, © 1979 by Harold Shaw Publishers.)

The first question asks you to observe many details from the text. You have to find specific elements in each dream and find the ways in which they're similar. You have to observe the reactions of Pharaoh, the court, and Joseph to the dreams.

The second and third questions require you to use the facts of the passage as a basis for drawing some conclusions. These questions search the actions, attitudes, and character traits of both Pharaoh and Joseph.

The fourth question builds on the observation and understanding questions as it asks you to extract a principle from Scripture and apply it to your own life.

The fifth question again asks you to observe facts from the passage, this time from the second part of the narrative. The sixth question asks you first to observe and then to understand by drawing some conclusions about Joseph's life.

The seventh and eighth questions direct the study into personal application again.

How does this kind of question sequence contribute to a good study and discussion? Primarily, it makes you discover the truth of the passage for yourself. Personal discovery is an important element in learning—we retain much more of what we find out for ourselves than we do if we hear it from someone else. And we retain longer and better what we actually *say;* therefore it is the study leader's role to *ask* the questions, not to answer them!

It's important to remember that all of the questions in inductive studies are important. Sometimes a group is tempted to skip the observation questions because the members think they're too obvious. Usually they won't be all that obvious, but if you think the observation questions in the guide are too easy and might offend the members of your group, you could reword those questions to provide more challenge.

If you skip the observation level in order to "get on to the really interesting stuff" you will considerably damage your goals. Here's why: First, observation questions provide a foundation on which to build understanding. Without them all of us would be tempted to use the Bible to prove our points and make it say something it doesn't.

In addition, by starting out on the observation level, you are providing an opportunity for the group to look at the passage together without assuming any prior knowledge on anyone's part. This means that a seminary graduate and an individual who has never opened a Bible before can study and learn together, without any feelings of inferiority or superiority. No one needs to feel left out or uniformed because, for the purposes of this study, you're all beginning at exactly the same place.

Working Out Together

By following the sequence of observation-understanding-application, a group can encompass just about as much variety in membership as you can imagine: young people and grandparents; Bible students and those just exploring the claims that Scripture makes; women and men; people with blue collars, pink collars, white collars, and even those with no collars at all! The inductive approach will unify an otherwise diverse group of people as they discover the truth of Scripture and allow it to work in their lives and change them in practical ways.

3

Leadership Styles— What Makes the Difference?

NOW WE ARE READY TO LOOK at the kind of leadership that makes the best use of this learning method.

Discussion leader A is comfortable, relaxed, and successful at helping her small group work together toward a deeper understanding of the Bible passage. Leader B is so nervous, blasé, and inflexible that the sessions get nowhere. What makes the difference between the two? Maybe the biggest difference is their understanding of the leader's role in a discussion Bible study. Let's take a look at some approaches that can cause problems.

Nervous Nellie was sure from the moment she found out she was going to lead that she couldn't possibly do it right. "I don't know nearly as much as Joan. She's had all those college courses," she frets. "And Ellen has taught Sunday school forever and she knows everything we're supposed to believe."

In fact Nellie often spends her preparation time worrying that she won't do a good job or won't know the "right" answers. By the time she gets to the study, she's so concerned about her own performance and her supposed inadequacies that she can't appreciate the content of the material or listen and respond to group members' questions and comments.

"This-is-old-stuff" Stella, on the other hand, has led Bible studies since Methuselah hung up his sandals. She used to spend a fair amount of time preparing the questions and praying for the group. Now she tends to look over the material the night before she's supposed to lead. She works on the assumption that all she has to do is read the questions off the page of the studyguide.

Stella has forgotten that she used to be challenged by Scripture study because she knew she could expect her own life to be changed. Now she expects very little and that's about what she gets. Unfortunately, so does the group.

Teacher Ted seems to be the opposite of Nellie and Stella. He believes it's not worth studying the Bible unless you can glean every last shade of meaning and thoroughly understand the historical background of each verse in the passage. He spends all week with his favorite concordance, topical index, Bible dictionary, and commentaries. He tends to rewrite all the questions in the studyguide and often changes the stated goal of the study.

He comes to the group with so much information that instead of asking discussion questions and working through the passage with the group, he ends up lecturing so that he can be sure everyone understands what's really important in the text. Group members often leave the study thinking that Ted knows a lot about the Bible and they know so little. Frequently they don't carry away anything new about the Scripture as it applies to their own lives.

Do you recognize yourself in any of these leaders? From time to time, we've all slipped into one or more of these caricatures of a Bible study leader. But we know we'd like to be different. The good news is that it doesn't take a college degree in Bible study methods, theology, or group dynamics to radically improve our leadership quotient.

4

Increasing Your LQ (Leadership Quotient)

THE BASIS FOR IMPROVING YOUR LEADERSHIP QUOTIENT is a renewed attitude and understanding about the leader's place and responsibility within the study group.

When we lead we need to remember that the group is not *my* group, but *our* group. A number of individuals have agreed to responsibly participate and build up the group, so we have shared ownership. Remembering that it's not *my* group enables me to let go of some of my defensiveness and uptightness. *I* am not responsible for creating a "perfect" group with perfect dynamics and perfect answers (likely to be perfectly dull!).

The leader should not aim to shape the thought patterns of the group or to manipulate the members into agreement on a point of belief. The leader has no hidden agenda to enforce on unsuspecting participants. Instead, the leader should help the group *discover together* the main points of a passage and then begin to understand how that section of Scripture applies to them individually.

This notion of co-ownership and shared responsibility is

strengthened by rotating leaders from week to week so that all members can be both leader-learners and participant-learners.

But the notion of co-ownership, as important as it is, does not free the leader from certain specific responsibilities. Whether it's the first or the fiftieth time we've led a study, we must be sure to do the following:

1/Spend some quality time in preparation so we're able to be true to the content of the passage (there's more detail on this aspect in the section "Preparing for the Workout").

2/Be willing to be confronted and changed by God's Word as we study and as we lead. We've seen that the goal of inductive study is to acquire a knowledge of Scripture so that we may understand and then find ourselves being remade in the image of Christ as we conform to the Word we've read. We should expect our beliefs, feelings, attitudes, and behavior to change as we live with and in God's Word. A Bible discussion leader is *not* someone who is already so mature that no more change is possible. Rather a leader points a little flashlight toward a much more powerful light—the glory, majesty, and love of God—and gives us a sense of what it means to be transformed in that love. Putting extra time into the study is one more reason why the leader can expect to see the greatest personal changes taking place.

3/Being a sensitive listener and observer as the discussion takes shape so that we can make it easier for participants to share their experiences and ask what might be, for them, hard questions (more on this in chapter 8, "Five Ways to Enhance Group Discussion").

4/Remember that we are learners as well as leaders, so expect good things to happen as the group works through the passage together.

5

Choosing
a Studyguide

ONE OF THE BEST TOOLS FOR HELPING your group achieve its goals is a well-chosen Bible studyguide. While a good studyguide does not do the leader's job for him or her or provide instant skills and techniques, it does provide a carefully-planned basis for studying the passage your group is interested in.

How do you go about choosing a guide when there are so many on the bookstore shelf? Think over the nature and goals of your particular group. For instance, your members may be primarily young Christians who are reading God's Word seriously for the first time. In that case, you'd probably turn to a study in the Gospels or a topical guide on the life of Christ to provide the spiritual milk young Christians and seekers need. None of us, of course, ever outgrows those dynamic accounts of "the Word made flesh."

Another type of guide that provides a high-interest entry into Bible study is the character study. It is exciting to meet Old or New Testament people and share their joys, sorrows, decisions, and problems. From these biblical biographies, we can learn what it means to be a person of God.

Perhaps a member of your group has raised a practical or doctrinal question that you would like to study together. One group's desire to know more about prayer resulted in some members writing a studyguide on the subject. Another group had questions about the nature of the church and chose to study Acts in order to get a first-hand picture of the early church to compare with present-day models.

If you want to sustain the interest level of your group, aim for balance and variety in your choice of studyguides. What have you been studying recently? If you've gone through several New Testament books, maybe it's time to use one of the excellent Old Testament studyguides. If your group has covered several of the basic books and you feel members have a good grasp of general biblical content, you might be ready to study a book such as Hebrews, Job, Romans, or Revelation. In general, these studies will presuppose more familiarity with the broader context of Scripture as well as some experience in discussion Bible study methods.

Just about any of these guides can be adapted to a variety of groups: campus studies, neighborhood groups meeting during the day, professionals studying together over a brown-bag lunch, evangelistic studies, mixed evening groups, and Sunday school classes.

6

Preparing for the Workout

"OH, THIS WILL BE EASY. The questions are all there; all I have to do is read them to the group, and we'll have a great Bible study."

Have you ever fallen into that trap, either because you found yourself in a time squeeze or because you were just plain lazy (it happens to the best of us)? I'm not about to tell you that no good can come out of a study when the leader is unprepared: surely once in nine hundred and eighty-seven times it will come out as well as you'd like it to. But, obviously, a quality discussion Bible study begins with some responsible preparation on the part of the leader. That does not mean, however, that you have to take a vacation day from work or eat frozen TV dinners every night for the week before you lead.

In most cases you'll know at least a week ahead of time when it's your turn to lead, so you can plan accordingly. Different people use different approaches. Some like to work a little on the study each day. Others like to carve out a long, uninterrupted block of time in which they can work through all the questions and background material at once. No matter what your personal taste and time schedule, here are some general guidelines you'll find helpful.

First, pray. Ask God to help you understand the passage and be willing to change your own actions or attitudes as his Word works in your life.

Pray for the individuals in your group—remembering their needs, giving thanks for their participation and for their contribution to your own life. It's also an invigorating challenge to look for new ways to pray, using the Scripture passage you're studying. Relate the passage to your own life and look for ways it can apply to and sustain other group members. For instance, if you were working with Psalm 1, you might thank God for the fact that he has planted you by a stream of living water and that you have seen definite growth and increasing maturity in your life. You might also thank him because Tom and Betty have turned away from a secular, spiritually unprofitable life and are seeking that same rootedness in God's Word.

Needless to say, panic praying at the last minute is better replaced by daily, more comfortable, unpressured conversations with God.

Second, read the passage several times in at least two different modern translations. Try to look at versions you don't normally use in your own devotional time. This will bring freshness to familiar passages and shed light on unfamiliar ones. The reading stage is a good time to make sure you can put the passage in the proper biblical context, especially if your group is just beginning a new book study. Knowing what has come before will help you understand new material.

It makes a big difference in the Gospels, for example, whether Jesus is speaking to his disciples or to the Pharisees. Whom did John the Baptist address as a "brood of vipers"? If the passage for a study doesn't make this kind of information clear, you'll need to look in the verses before and after it. You might ask yourself questions like: Who's talking or writing? Is there a specific audience? Is a question being answered or a main theme being supported? In the historical narratives, especially in the Old Testament, be careful to separate the good guys from the bad guys.

Often, to get a more complete picture of the text, you'll want to do some extra digging for information. But how much background work should you do? You'll probably want to read more if your group is just beginning a new study on a Bible book or character than if you're already halfway through the studyguide when it's your time to lead. The rule of thumb is to look up whatever you have questions about as you're reading the passage. Then use that information *if* you're asked during the discussion. Be careful, because the more you know and feel you *must* share, the more likely you are to fall into the "teacher Ted" model. Remember the group's goal is to discover together, not to listen to a lecture. Be sure to look up any words you're not familiar with; there's a good chance that if you don't know what they mean, others won't either. (For reference tools, see the Suggested Reading List at the end of this book.)

After you've spent some time with the passage in a couple of different translations, try to summarize what's been said (or, in the case of a narrative, what has happened). Decide for yourself what the main point of the passage is. Thinking through the passage *before* you start using the guide will help you understand the Scripture you're studying. With that background, you'll be able to evaluate and use the discussion questions more carefully and comfortably.

Some groups decide not to study ahead of time so that the questions are fresh. This approach allows for a little more spontaneity in the actual discussion time. Other groups agree to have everyone work through the questions during the week and come with written answers. This alternative allows more time for discussing the understanding and application levels of the Bible study. If you've chosen the second approach, remember that participants need to be free from having their noses (and thinking patterns) glued to the words they've already written down. It's very possible to get a new idea in the middle of the discussion!

Now it's time to turn to the studyguide.

In most cases you will find that the studyguide you're using has more questions than your group can answer in forty-five minutes or an hour. Part of the leader's job is to choose the seven to nine questions which will best help the group move through the passage on the observation and understanding levels and then motivate participants to apply the main point of the Scripture to their own lives. This means, of course, balancing all three kinds of questions. The title or subheading of the study can help you as you choose questions; it usually indicates where the studyguide writer sees the discussion going. Also, a quick look at the application questions—usually placed at the end of the study—can give you a sense of the goal for the week.

Look for questions that not only provide a good balance and move the discussion toward the main point, but also invite multiple responses. Most people hesitate to respond to a question that can be answered in a single word or that has only one correct answer. Perhaps we feel it's too obvious and therefore childish, or maybe we feel negative toward such a teacher-pupil programmed response. For instance, in a study on Joseph's early life in Egypt, this question, "What problems and tensions did Joseph face as he fulfilled his responsibilities in Potiphar's house?" allows for several responses and offers more scope for discussion than a question such as, "What sin did Joseph avoid?"

Some questions may seem to be particularly appropriate for your group. Members may be especially interested in the theological ramifications or the political significance of a section of Scripture, while these items might not be of primary importance to another group and would merely bog them down. So you need to assess your group's interests as you work through the questions.

Once you've chosen the seven to nine questions that provide a clear pathway to the goal of the study, star or highlight them in the studyguide. This trick will help you keep track of your most important questions without having your head buried in the guide during the discussion time. It's also a good idea to jot down timing notes in the margin. Mark the questions you plan to reach by the time you are one-third and two-thirds through the study. This will keep you from getting bogged down and give you a sense of timing once the discussion gets going.

It often helps to practice saying the key questions out loud (preferably *not* on the commuter train or in the supermarket!). You may want to reword a question or two so it feels more comfortable coming out of your mouth. However, be careful not to change the original intent of the question.

Finally, before you've finished studying, make sure you understand the sort of answers each question is looking for. Check to see that you have grasped the main point(s) of the study and that you understand how the questions are getting you there. Note, however, that this does not mean there is only one right answer to a question or that it is your job to see that all members of the group agree on every point.

With continuing prayer and a quiet confidence that God knows what he's doing and has promised the Holy Spirit as your teacher-leader, you're ready to lead the study! What could be easier?

7

Interacting with the Group

IN SOME WAYS THE LEADER OF A DISCUSSION GROUP is like the coach of a sports team. His role is to enable individual group members to contribute their best and to feel part of the team. At the same time, of course, the leader has a responsibility to the Bible passage—to see that the discussion stays on track and that the points and questions raised are valid. The leader also sets the tone of the group, creating an atmosphere in which all feel free to learn, share, change, and grow.

The quality of interaction within the group depends a lot on the quality of discussion and follow-up questions the leader asks, as well as his or her attitude toward the question-asking process. For instance, if the leader asks the first question in the guide and expects a single answer (perhaps leaving the impression that there is only one right answer and/or we have to move right along or we can't possibly finish this study on time), then the group will likely respond in kind: giving a single, often superficial, "pat" answer. In this scenario, the leader then asks the second question, perhaps not even looking up from the studyguide, and moves right along as soon as another "right" answer is given. The leader's goal of getting all the questions answered may be met, but little else will have taken place— certainly not a thoughtful discussion.

A more fruitful exchange is one in which two or more members respond to the first question the leader asks. Usually at least one of those responses will elicit a comment or question from yet another member of the group.

In the first scene, we can picture the leader throwing a ball to a player in the circle who then returns it to her. The leader then throws the ball out again to another player who also dutifully returns it. The individual players might as well be walled off from each other.

But in the second picture, while the leader initiates the game of catch, there's no rule that says she has to put her hands back on the ball between each player's attempt at catching and throwing. No walls separate the group members and several can get into the game at the same time. This kind of group interaction produces group ownership. All the members are interested in the content of the study and in each other's insights and responses. They listen to each other, ask questions to clarify or expand a point, and evaluate their own thoughts, feelings, and experiences. This dynamic structure demands that all listen and all participate. It is the leader's role to sense when a discussion has progressed as far as it can profitably go. Then it's time for the next question as the study moves toward its application goals.

8

Five Ways
to Enhance
Group Discussion

IN WHAT WAYS CAN YOU HELP the flow of discussion on the study topic?

First, don't answer your own questions and don't be afraid of silence. After you ask a question, be prepared to wait a few seconds before you get responses. This may be hard at first because you'll be tempted to rush in and fill the gap with your own words. Remember that people need time to zero in on the passage the question refers to (especially if they haven't had adequate preparation time) and to see how the text gives them an answer. They need time to think through their own experiences, combine information, and express it in words. Some people even have to work up their courage to say *anything* in a group.

Sometimes people hesitate because the question itself is not clear. You may need to reword the question for the group so that it is understandable and comfortably phrased. Thoughtful preparation time will help you avoid unclear questions most of the time.

Most often a period of silence (although it may seem to go on forever) is a productive, working time and should not be cut off too quickly. If first aid efforts become necessary, however, try asking a secondary question dealing with one aspect of the original question to help revive the dialogue.

As discussion leaders we need to remember that our role as a participant is limited by our role as a leader. In one sense we give up some freedom when it's our turn to lead, and that includes the freedom to open our mouths. Unfortunately, one of the single greatest failings of leaders is that they talk too much (I'm speaking from painful personal experience!). How can you avoid that? Try only asking questions. Don't make a single declarative statement while you're leading the study. You may go home with cramps in your jaws, but you will have learned more than twenty books could tell you about the secrets of being a good leader.

Second, remember that leading a discussion group is something like conducting an orchestra. You need to keep track both of time and content throughout the study. You don't want the discussion to get bogged down so you never get past question two in the studyguide. Neither do you want to shoot the questions out so fast that there's no real discussion and only a superficial understanding of the material. Timing cues previously jotted down in the margin of your studyguide will help here.

When you glance at your watch and see that the group has used up half the study time and you're not to the halfway point in your list of questions (and remember that the application questions often placed at the end of the study will take longer), then it's time for you to pick up the baton and increase the tempo. You'll find that it's not too hard to say, "We're having a good discussion on this point, but I'm afraid we'll have to continue it after the study or we'll miss a couple of important points further on." Because the study is a corporate enterprise, the members will probably be sensitive to this need, especially if leadership is rotated. When your group knows the benefits of using the inductive system of study, they'll be more than coop-erative.

Third, learn to deal effectively with incorrect or off-base answers. How do you do this? Not the way I did—by telling the poor erring soul she couldn't *possibly* believe that. I not only shut off all discussion (who wants to suggest an answer when they're going to be told they're absolutely wrong?), but also effectively silenced this woman for several weeks to come.

One simple and much more tactful way of dealing with such a situation is to ask for other responses to the same question: "Tim, is that how you understand the meaning of this verse?" Follow this up by asking someone else to think through the resulting application of each interpretation. For example, "What difference would it make in your attitude toward Jesus (or the way you treat your family members) if you understood the verse this way?"

Fourth, encourage balanced participation. You'll find that there are both tubas and piccolos in your group. Your goal is to direct the tuba player so that he doesn't overshadow every-body else, and at the same time to encourage the piccolo player to make his own valuable contribution. By the way, it's often the shy, quiet ones in the group who have the most profound things to say. (I know—I'm a tuba!)

How do you keep your talky friend from overpowering the study and still keep him or her as a friend? One suggestion would be to have him or her read this book in order to be both a better leader and a better participant.

You can also use a couple of tricks in your physical setting that usually do their silent work quite well. Avoid making eye contact with the talky members, and work on eye contact with those who are usually quiet. If it won't put him or her on the spot, direct a question to a more retiring member. If you're sitting around in a circle, try sitting next to the more vocal member. This accomplishes a couple of things: in this position, it's almost impossible to have eye contact, and you'll be close enough to gently put out a restraining hand as a silent signal for him or her to give someone else a chance.

Some groups have agreed that those with quick minds and active jaw muscles will count to twenty (silently) before answering a question. At the same time, these individuals are encouraged to work on active listening. This means that the one who finds talking easier puts aside the next three brilliant statements he's about to make and really listens to another's contribution. Then, instead of jumping in with his own ideas, he asks a follow-up question that draws out that other group member.

Besides encouraging talkative members to discipline themselves, the leader must sensitively encourage quieter group members to contribute. Achieving balanced participation is a sure sign that your group is healthy and in shape. Sometimes the direct approach works best: "OK, Ralph, I understand your position on this subject now, but I'm wondering what Karen has to say about it."

One skilled leader I know brings nickels to the meeting and distributes two to each member. Each time you talk, you "spend" one of your nickels, perhaps tossing it into the central dish. The economy of the discussion dictates that when your supply is gone, you have to wait until everyone has spent his or her nickels and the pile is redistributed before you can talk again. This gimmick underscores the responsibility of all members to contribute to the discussion.

If you do this group dynamics exercise just once, the group has a referent even when the nickels aren't present. "Sally, you've already spent your nickels," or, "Henry's hoarding his nickels again." The point is to emphasize group ownership and responsibility in participation and self-control. That burden should not rest solely on the leader's shoulders.

Some members may be unusually quiet. Perhaps they are not natural talkers; perhaps they are shy, new members. They may not feel they know enough to speak up, or they may be bringing with them problems they're not yet ready to share.

Rule number one is, don't force anyone to contribute. Your goal is to create an atmosphere of trust and freedom so that eventually everyone will feel comfortable participating.

It's often easier to respond to an observation question than to one that asks for personal sharing on the application level. So, if the silent newcomer hasn't made a contribution for a few weeks, you might ask him to read part of the passage or to answer one of the observation questions which have several answers in the text. But don't put him on the spot; proceed with TLC. It usually happens that once a person has said *something* in the group, he or she finds it easier to make another contribution.

There are no pat formulas for getting everyone in the group involved. However, caring and concern, sensitive listening, watchful eyes, appropriate facial expressions, and body language all can help.

Fifth, care for emotionally-needy people during the discussion. Sometimes you will encounter genuine problem people in your study. These are members who constantly draw the group's attention and energy away from the passage and toward themselves. Often they are going through an emotional crisis or facing difficulties in their home or work situation. It is important to remember that a Bible study discussion group should offer love and care, but it is not a therapy session. Whenever possible, one or more members of the group should spend time with the hurting person outside the study time, giving him or her the extra support needed. This caring partner(s) can also sit next to the problem person in the study, helping him maintain self-control when necessary by the light pressure of a hand on an arm.

If a person is truly disrupting the study (and these times are indeed rare), most groups find it best for the leader or a friend to take the member into another room where they can talk or pray. The group, meanwhile, might pause to pray for the person and then continue with the study. The hurting member can then return to a normal, rather than an awkward, group situation.

Again, such situations will not be standard fare in Bible study groups, but they can occur. Keep the good of the group in mind while caring for the individual.

9

Dealing with Problems in the Text

As we're thinking through things that could possibly go wrong in the discussion study, we should look at textual problems. Actually, though, these end up being problems *people* have with the passage, rather than problems in the text itself.

Sometimes a group member will ask a question or make a comment that indicates a simple lack of information or comprehension. Or someone will remember a verse somewhere else that seems to contradict what you've just read. Most of the time a careful look at the verse in its proper context will resolve the problem. Having a good Bible dictionary on hand will allow you to look up a few key terms if there seems to be a misunderstanding or a lack of knowledge. In addition, members who are more familiar with the broader context of Scripture might be able to put the specific verse into that larger perspective.

Often we come to the Bible with preconceived notions of what a passage says. Sometimes these mindsets come from our general cultural background. (It took me a long time to accept that the Bible does *not* say, "God helps those who help themselves.") Our denominational or doctrinal position can also predispose us to read every passage in that light alone.

Personally, I have to guard my reactions against a text when I don't like what I think God is saying to me through it. I don't like to give up my comfortable habits, whether they are thoughts or actions, and I often resist the changes God's Spirit wants to work in me. His way of leading me to maturity in Christ is sometimes rather uncomfortable, and I want to avoid discomfort or downright pain. My anger, defensiveness, or attempts to "explain away" a passage are pretty good clues that I need to look within myself before arguing with Scripture.

Often your discussion will go more smoothly, especially in a group unfamiliar with the Bible, if you all use the same modern translation. Two of the most widely accepted translations for Bible study discussion groups are the *Revised Standard Version* and the *New International Version*. Inexpensive copies of these are available for group purchase.

If your group chooses to use a variety of versions of the Bible, be sure to use *translations* and not paraphrases. For instance, editions such as *The Living Bible, The Amplified Bible,* or the version by J.B. Phillips can be meaningful for devotional reading, but they are not adequate for serious study. And as meaningful as the *King James Version* is to those who have grown up with it, its outdated language (1611) prevents it from being the best choice for a study Bible.

Problems can arise over the difference in word choice among translations used by your group. If this happens, examine the *context* of the word in each version. Many words have more than one valid meaning and translators choose which meaning seems to fit the context best.

Some textual problems are harder to resolve. For example, certain passages of Scripture can be validly understood in more than one way. If that were not so, we wouldn't even have the word "denomination." When your group comes to such a passage, try to look fairly at the various possible interpretations. It helps to hold the attitude that there are many things we can't know for sure, and that our responsibility is to try to see what all the possibilities are. I would hasten to add, however, that so much of Scripture is straightforward and clear in its message—telling of God's love and the meaning of Christ's death and mediation for us, as well as the responses we should make to this message—that it would take a long time for us to run out of opportunities for positive growth through Bible study.

When your group has a question about the text, use this opportunity to improve your skills in Bible study. During the week, employ all the tools at your disposal: Bible dictionaries and handbooks, concordances, commentaries, maps, etc. (See Suggestions for Further Reading at the end of this book). Then report back your findings.

In one group, members keep a running list of thorny questions and items they would like more information on. Then, about once a quarter, they invite one of their pastors to share a pot-luck supper in exchange for being put on the "hot seat." They've found that this quiz-the-pastor night not only helps them understand the Scripture better, but also builds up a communication bridge between the institutional church and their small study group.

In the end, we need to remember that there simply are not answers to all questions. I don't know why God made us so that our funny heads could think up more problems and questions than we could accept solutions for. Perhaps it was to remind us that ultimately he is the Truth, and we are, and always will be, dependent on him for the final answers.

At times group members will have to agree to disagree, especially as they discover some denominational differences. Usually the different belief systems can each find support in Scripture, and the question will almost never be crucial to faith. The leader should help group members understand that they don't have to decide which point of view is right and which is wrong, and that no one needs to be afraid to hold a well-supported, minority interpretation.

This is a good place for a reminder that a discussion Bible study does not function so that some individuals can persuade everyone else to join their church (or their particular ideological crusade). For the most part, Bible study groups are made up of active church members who participate in a lay Bible study in addition to their commitment to a body of believers who worship together and sit under solid preaching of the Word. As new members come to our group, some will likely be looking for a church in which they can feel at home. Certainly invitations from members to visit their churches are proper, but proselytizing is not. The focus for us is the Word of God and how we may learn together to appropriate it into our lives and then share it with others.

10

Building Up
Your Prayer Muscles

PRAYING TOGETHER CAN KEEP your group healthy, but if you don't approach it with the same care and attention as the rest of the study, one of the most exciting times in your Bible study can turn into the most awkward and uncomfortable period.

I've been in some groups when Samantha Jones felt "led" to pray for everything under the sun—and she did without taking a breath! By the time she was through, those of us who hadn't fallen asleep felt we had nothing to add to her prayer encyclopedia.

In other groups, members pray independently, throwing their separate requests up to God. Bill asks God to help him be more regular in his personal Bible study. Mary follows that prayer by asking God to strengthen her mother's weak knee. Then Jean prays for her new pastor. This hodgepodge results in the feeling that we might as well have been standing back-to-back because we are each trying to get God's attention for ourselves, instead of working out together.

I've also participated in some groups where the leader has closed the study by saying, "Well, it's time to pray; let's just go around the circle." Sometimes I didn't feel like praying when my turn came so I just mumbled something that sounded sufficiently religious and socially acceptable. This circle approach is particularly hard on the visitor, new Christian, or non-Christian in the group. Some feel so much negative peer pressure that they never return to the study.

With a little thought, training, and cooperation, the worst of times can also be the best of times. One approach that has worked well for many groups is known as "conversational prayer." (Rosalind Rinker, as well as others, has written extensively on this means of praying together; her books are included in *Suggestions for Further Reading* at the end of this book.)

Basically, conversational prayer encourages a dialogue among all those present, including God. It assumes that God is not a towering mountain of stone or fire who must only be addressed in the most formal and stuffy language, but that he is a caring, loving Father who wishes to develop a personal relationship with us.

Realizing that you are also participating in a conversation with the rest of the members of your group is just as important as freely entering into a dialogue with God. Remember—all of you have come into God's presence together.

Talking together to God has several implications. First, we listen to each other, trying to be sensitive to the feelings of the person praying. And then, as in any good conversation, several of us will respond to that prayer, staying on the same topic, affirming and encouraging the one who has just prayed and perhaps sharing our own desires or needs on that same subject. We remain on that topic as long as it seems appropriate, wait a few seconds to see if there are any additions, and then move on to our next concern.

In conversational prayer, our prayers will tend to be shorter than the typical formal prayer. Probably each of us will pray several times as new subjects are introduced.

Rosalind Rinker suggests an order or progression as we pray conversationally and topically. Perhaps it will help you and your Bible study group.

1/Be aware that the Lord Jesus is with you and offer him worship and praise.

2/Give him thanks for what he has done and is doing in the world, your community, your family, and in your own life. Thank him for himself and for each other.

3/Pray for those present, including yourself. These prayers will include confession, acceptance of forgiveness, affirmation of each other, and the willingness to receive love from each other and from God. Miss Rinker calls these prayers, "Help me Lord."

4/Pray for others, including those not present, exercising the power of intercession. This fourth category Miss Rinker calls, "Help my brother." When we pray in this way, we are, in effect, sharing our love and God's love with others.

This suggested order is helpful because first we center on Jesus, expressing our gratitude to him. Then we recognize our own sins and accept his forgiveness, preparing us to ask confidently for his gifts for ourselves and others.

When several people pray on one subject, affirming and supporting each other in worship, thanksgiving, confession, and request, there can be powerful emotional and spiritual consequences. We begin to feel a part of each other. After hearing verbal expressions of others' love for us, we begin to discover that we care for them as well (perhaps more deeply than we thought possible). Our level of friendship and fellowship grows, and our spiritual health, both individually and collectively, improves. As we learn more about praying for others and become more diligent in doing so, we rest in the knowledge that they are supporting us in their prayers as well. We are all growing together in the unity of the love and power of our Lord.

If we diligently pursue it, the discipline of prayer can become the capstone of a challenging, growing Bible study experience as well as a monitor of our spiritual fitness.

11

Introducing Others to Christ

SOME OF THE PEOPLE WHO START to come regularly to your study will not have met or made a commitment to Jesus Christ. That's just great, because it gives you the privilege, perhaps, of performing that introduction.

Bible study groups are not set up with an evangelist-in-residence. Rather, each of us is responsible to be ready and willing to share with our friends when they are ready to hear more about what it's like to have a relationship with Jesus.

What's involved in this process? First, we need to recognize that God *wants* our friends to be his friends. His Spirit is actively working in them to deepen their yearning and receptivity to him. His Spirit is also available to us to increase our faith and love. And as we study and pray together, he will be in our midst, creating an atmosphere of mutual respect, trust, and love.

Not only do we have the promise of God's presence with us, but we also have his Word, the Bible, which is the center of attention in our study. It's the place to go to find answers to hard questions and discover who Jesus is and why we would want to follow him.

In combination with God's presence and his Word, our own attitude makes it possible for us to share information about Jesus with others: we come to the group willing to be friends with others in that room. We are willing to trust them and to speak, act, and respond to them in ways that will help them know we are trustworthy and maybe even fun or challenging to know. A discussion Bible study group is more than a place where we can openly examine the claims of Scripture. It's a place where relationships grow.

Deciding that Jesus is trustworthy, that he would be a good friend, that he is worth committing one's self to and following as Savior and Lord is usually a process that occurs over a period of time. Our job is to reflect Christ by sharing our own life—warts and all—with those we are getting to know in our group. Spending time with people outside the study, getting to know them, and showing them that we appreciate them for who they are is an important part of this process. We need to be especially sensitive to the person who is asking lots of questions and to the ones we personally invited to our study group.

Be ready to share your faith, probably a piece at a time, as people are ready to hear. Becky Pippert has said, "A secret to more effective personal evangelism is discovering the art of story-telling—learning how to tell His story and your own story." In sharing with others we should be able to identify the crucial elements of our belief and then relate those beliefs in our own story of a personal relationship with Christ, always sticking to simple, natural language. You may want to read *Finders Keepers*, by Dee Brestin, for a detailed explanation of how you can lead another person to Christ.

12

Keeping the Group Running Smoothly

To keep your group functioning smoothly, you'll find that some members will need to share some responsibility in keeping the group healthy. In addition to attending, participating, and taking a turn at leading, here are some examples of those necessary jobs in study groups.

Your group will have decided on a consistent meeting place, such as a church, school room, office or conference room, or one member's house that is centrally located. Or perhaps you've decided to rotate among group members' houses. Whatever the location, someone needs to be responsible for making the arrangements and getting in touch with group members in case of a last-minute change of plans.

If some of the members have preschool children, you need a nursery coordinator. While some groups assume individuals will arrange for their own babysitting needs, most groups which have young mothers attending (or have the potential for such membership) try to make group arrangements. Usually it works best when the sitting facilities are not located in the same place as the study group. Possibilities include another member's home in the neighborhood or the nursery of a local church. Because nursery availability is a privilege for all the members of the group, it seems like a fair suggestion that all individuals contribute to the fee whether or not they have children. (Remember, the alternative to a nursery is missing out on the active participation of some worthwhile people or having a study that's constantly interrupted by the laughing or crying of one or more little ones.) The nursery coordinator's thoughtful organization of these details will let a prospective new member know she's welcome and that you've given some thought to her needs.

Every so often the group will need to decide on a new topic for study and choose a new guide. The process will be sped along if one or two members visit the local Christian bookstore, pick out several guides that seem to fit the group's needs, and report back. Once the group has made its choice someone can order the correct number of studyguides from the bookstore (at least three weeks in advance to allow for shipping!).

Sooner or later an informal "core group" will evolve to pick up these sorts of responsibilities. While in no way diminishing the concept of shared or corporate ownership of the group, these few individuals will make a special commitment to the long-range health and functioning of your group.

In addition to watching over the mechanics, the core group will also serve another special need. They will meet together (perhaps once a month) to pray for group members, troubleshoot any potential problems, review goals, and evaluate the growth of the group. This is not a ruling class, but a caring group which will initiate ideas and programs and take on extra responsibility. You'll probably find that the composition of this informal smaller group changes from year to year, depending on individual commitments to job, family, church, etc. Wouldn't it be great if, sooner or later, all the group members would take a turn at carrying some of these responsibilities? Then you'd really be working out together!

13

Busting at
the Seams?

IF THE LIVING ROOM WHERE YOU'RE MEETING is beginning to feel a little cramped, or if you have so many group members that the shy ones shrink into the wallpaper and don't venture a response to most questions, congratulations! Your group has reached that painful and exciting time when you're ready to divide.

It's likely that everyone will have some negative feelings about this move. Perhaps we have a problem with the notion of "splitting" at all—it may carry a connotation of divisiveness for us.

But an even greater barrier to dividing the group is the good feeling of fellowship that has grown during the year—the friends you've made, the honest sharing you've grown to expect. You may think back to how the first four or five of you struggled along for weeks or months before others came. You may remember feeling a certain reserve or hesitation until you got to know and trust each other. You see quite a difference when you compare those experiences with the vitality of your group in the past two or three months.

And now I'm suggesting you start at the beginning again? That's *exactly* the game plan, and ultimately it will yield positive results, even though it may be painful right now. After all, our goal is to multiply, and groups reproduce just like the one-celled critters in Biology 101—by dividing.

A rule of the thumb that has worked for many groups is this: create new groups of about six people, including at least one person who has led studies and one who is ready to take on some leadership responsibilities. If you start with about six, you are giving yourselves room to double within a year of your first meeting together.

"But how can we divide?" you ask. "We're all so close!" One good way to approach the problem is for the core group to brainstorm a couple of possible ways to divide. Perhaps members fit into obvious geographical groups. Maybe some prefer a morning meeting while others would opt for early afternoon or evening studies.

After brainstorming, share the possible solutions with the group as a whole—carefully explaining the reasons for creating another group. You can probably expect some negative response in the beginning, but if you are convinced about your decision and use patience and tact, you'll see the groups divide, multiply, and grow.

Remember, friendships formed between members will not wither because you now have two groups. If real relationships have developed, it's because people have also shared with each other outside of Bible study time. That reaching out can still go on—and it should.

You may want to suggest that the two groups, including the new members they'll be counting on, plan to have a joint Christmas salad lunch and another fellowship time in the spring. Making some definite plans *now* for a reunion usually helps ease the transition.

Often leaders of the two new groups will want to meet together to encourage each other and exchange ideas during the year (perhaps more frequently at first, until they feel their groups are stable).

The groups may study the same material. However, many groups that have divided find that studying two different books or topics opens more opportunities to invite new people; they now have a choice of subjects to study—right in their own neighborhood or office or dorm.

Some groups decide to meet in a home equipped to handle two groups (living room and basement family room for example) and share a common babysitter in a neighboring house or church nursery. As good as this idea may sound, in practice it has not proved successful. Problems arise with getting the groups started on time, and there is often cross-visiting which slows down the creation of a new group identity.

Groups that have tried this approach offer these tips: if you want to share a babysitter, fine, but have the groups meet in two different homes so there won't be any confusion about who belongs where.

If you're discouraged about the prospects of dividing, just remember that we're all called to share the good news of God's truth. By dividing we can make it possible for more people to get in on the joy of discovering and applying God's Word. This process of expanding our relationships and sharing in the lives of other believers can also be an impetus to greater growth in our faith. Just as human families reproduce themselves into successive generations, so members of your Bible study can initiate and develop other groups that will, in turn, begin to grow into maturity and fitness in Christ.

Evaluation and Checklists

The process of setting goals and reviewing growth is important, both for individual members and for the study group. The following suggested checklists can help you and your group evaluate your participation. If several people will be discussing the points, try having each participant answer the questions before you meet together.

Personal Checklist
1/Do you have a daily quiet time? What do you generally do during such a time?
2/Do you study the passage before coming to Bible study in the weeks when you're not leading?
3/Besides the studyguide, what other Christian books do you read?
4/Do you pray for the group and individual members during the week?

Group Checklist

1/Is your Bible study really a discussion Bible study? (Is there discussion? Is it centered on the text you are studying?)

2/As you observe your group discussion, what would you say are the elements of good study and good discussion?

3/Evaluate the honesty and openness of group members. To what would you attribute their freedom, or lack of it?

4/What are the special assets of your group?

5/Do you feel free to bring a non-Christian friend? Why or why not? If you have brought someone to the group, what was his or her response?

6/How do members of your group serve each other? To what extent are the members in touch with each other between group meetings?

7/Do you and/or others meet to pray for the group during the week? With what result?

8/Are the active discussion leaders encouraging and training others to lead? How?

9/How do group members help each other in areas such as discipleship, personal Bible study, sharing their faith, etc.?

10/To what extent do group members serve in the community and their local churches?

11/How has your group changed during this year? What changes would you like to see in the future?

12/What are your goals for the group? What specific actions, activities, and changes are required to meet these goals?

13/What are you willing to do for the group next year? Next week? Today?

One last question: Now that you've read the book and answered these questions, what ideas do you have that you'd like to put into action?

Suggestions for Further Reading

Reference Materials

Howley, G.D.C., Bruce, F.F., and Ellison, H.L., eds. *The New Layman's Bible: Commentary in One Volume*. Grand Rapids: Zondervan, 1979.

Douglas, J.D., ed. *The New Bible Dictionary*. Wheaton, Ill.: Tyndale, 1982.

Elwell, Walter, ed. *The Shaw Pocket Bible Handbook*. Wheaton, Ill.: Shaw, 1984.

Strong's Exhaustive Concordance of the Bible (King James). Nashville: Abingdon.

Strong's Exhaustive Concordance of the Bible (NASB). Nashville: Holman.

(You may wish to use a concordance based on the Bible you use, e.g. the NIV. Visit your local Christian bookstore for a full selection.)

Leadership and Group Skills

The Fisherman's Net (a free resource quarterly for leaders), Wheaton, Ill.: Shaw.

Griffin, Em. *Getting Together: A Guide for Good Groups*. Downers Grove, Ill.: InterVarsity, 1982.

Hunt, Gladys. *You Can Start a Bible Study Group: Making Friends, Changing Lives.* Wheaton, Ill.: Shaw, 1984.

Nicholas, Ron et al. *Good Things Come in Small Groups.* Downers Grove, Ill.: InterVarsity, 1985.

Sharing Christ

Brestin, Dee. *Finders Keepers.* Wheaton, Ill.: Shaw, 1983.

Lum, Ada. *How to Begin an Evangelistic Bible Study,* Downers Grove, Ill.: InterVarsity, 1979.

Stott, John R. W. *Becoming a Christian* (booklet). Downers Grove, Ill.: InterVarsity.

Stott, John R. W. *Being a Christian* (booklet). Downers Grove, Ill.: InterVarsity.

Personal Growth

Munger, Robert B. *My Heart—Christ's Home* (booklet). Downers Grove, Ill.: InterVarsity, 1979.

Quiet Time. Downers Grove, Ill.: InterVarsity, 1979.

Trobisch, Walter. *Martin Luther's Quiet Time* (booklet). Downers Grove, Ill.: InterVarsity, 1979.

Prayer

Fromer, Margaret & Keyes, Sharrel. *Let's Pray Together* (a Fisherman Bible studyguide). Wheaton, Ill.: Shaw, 1974.

Paterson, Janet. *How to Pray Together* (booklet). Downers Grove, Ill.: InterVarsity, 1979.

Rinker, Rosalind. *Communicating Love through Prayer.* Grand Rapids: Zondervan, 1979.

Rinker, Rosalind. *Conversational Prayer.* Waco, Tex.: Word, 1979.

Rinker, Rosalind. *Prayer: Conversing with God.* Grand Rapids: Zondervan, 1979.

Rinker, Rosalind. *Praying Together.* Grand Rapids: Zondervan, 1980.

Finding a Direction for Your Bible Study Group

"What shall we study next?" is a typical question heard in a Bible study group which has just completed a studyguide together. Members may have all kinds of suggestions based on their own personal needs and interests, but choosing may not be all that easy.

Your list of long-term criteria may look something like this:
Studyguides must
—meet group members' spiritual needs
—fit in with members' interests
—cover a balanced range of Bible themes, authors, characters, emphases, writing styles
—explore major areas of Christian life and belief
—increase in complexity and depth as the group matures

A group that is stuck in a rigid curriculum may lose members' interest along the way. On the other hand, if group members impulsively choose studyguides based on immediate needs and interests, how are they to fulfill the other criteria adequately?

The *Fisherman Study Circle* (see next page) provides an alternative. Here are helpful but flexible guidelines that will enable your group to find the best direction for their study. As you scan the Fisherman Bible Studyguides program arranged in the Study Circle, you'll see four categories: *Core studies, Bible book studies, Character studies,* and *Topical studies.* All of these follow the inductive method of questions and discussion of the Bible text.

Note the Core studies at the center of the Circle. These basic Book and Topical studies have been developed for beginning groups to provide a foundation for further study and growth. Beyond the core level, your group can branch out into the other three areas, perhaps alternating between Bible book, Character, and Topical studies to give needed variety and change of pace. More challenging studies are marked with an asterisk (*) and are planned for experienced groups with a firm understanding of Bible content.

The Fisherman Study Circle

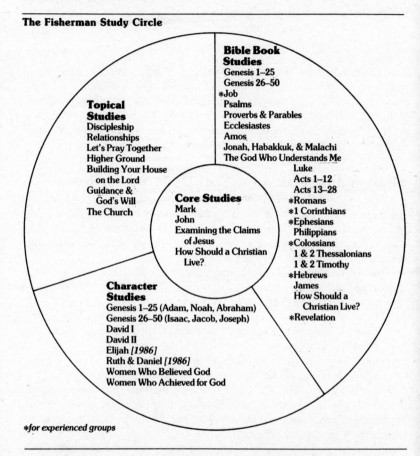

Bible Book Studies
Genesis 1–25
Genesis 26–50
*Job
Psalms
Proverbs & Parables
Ecclesiastes
Amos
Jonah, Habakkuk, & Malachi
The God Who Understands Me
Luke
Acts 1–12
Acts 13–28
*Romans
*1 Corinthians
*Ephesians
Philippians
*Colossians
1 & 2 Thessalonians
1 & 2 Timothy
*Hebrews
James
How Should a Christian Live?
*Revelation

Topical Studies
Discipleship
Relationships
Let's Pray Together
Higher Ground
Building Your House on the Lord
Guidance & God's Will
The Church

Core Studies
Mark
John
Examining the Claims of Jesus
How Should a Christian Live?

Character Studies
Genesis 1–25 (Adam, Noah, Abraham)
Genesis 26–50 (Isaac, Jacob, Joseph)
David I
David II
Elijah [1986]
Ruth & Daniel [1986]
Women Who Believed God
Women Who Achieved for God

*for experienced groups

By planning with the Study Circle you will cover the major areas of the Bible and Christian life in a systematic and balanced way, grow in maturity as a group, and learn to study God's Word in more depth.

You will find a detailed listing of the Fisherman Bible Studyguide Series on the last page of this book.

To Meet Your Other Bible Study Needs . . .

For Adults:
Personal Bible Studyguides: Daily studies for individual use combining prayer, Scripture reading, inductive questions, commentary notes by trusted biblical scholars, personal response, and memorization.
Carpenter Studyguides: Bible study *plus,* for small groups within the church. Includes worship, prayer, outreach, relationship-building, and more. Groups use members' handbooks as well as leaders' handbooks containing many additional ideas for enhancing the life of the group.

For Young People:
Young Fisherman Bible Studyguides: Inductive Bible studies for junior high and high school groups in Christian schools, Sunday schools, youth groups, camps, and CCD programs. The student edition contains thought-provoking questions and humorous illustrations; the teacher edition includes background information, and a reduced student page with side-by-side notes for each question.

You can learn more about all of the Shaw studyguides by obtaining a free **Harold Shaw Publishers BIBLE STUDY CATALOG:** a 32-page illustrated booklet describing each of the nearly 70 studyguides in the Fisherman, Young Fisherman, Carpenter, and Personal Bible Studyguides series. It's a helpful planning tool.
Also available is **The Fisherman's Net,** a free resource quarterly for Bible study leaders.

All studyguides and materials are available at your local bookstore or from Harold Shaw Publishers, Box 567, Wheaton, Illinois 60189.

Fisherman Bible Studyguides

WORKING OUT TOGETHER: Keeping Your Group in Shape, by Sharrel Keyes. A resource book for this series. *263-0*

YOU CAN START A BIBLE STUDY GROUP: Making Friends, Changing Lives, by Gladys Hunt. A resource book for this series. *974-0*

GENESIS 1-25: Walking with God, 15 studies by Margaret Fromer & Sharrel Keyes. *297-5*

GENESIS 26-50: Called by God, 15 studies by Margaret Fromer & Sharrel Keyes. *298-3*

DAVID: Man after God's Own Heart, Vol. I, 12 studies by Robbie Castleman. *164-2*

DAVID: Man after God's Own Heart, Vol. II, 12 studies by Robbie Castleman. *165-0*

JOB: God's Answer to Suffering, 13 studies by Ron Klug. *430-7*

PSALMS: A Guide to Prayer & Praise, 15 studies by Ron Klug. *699-7*

PROVERBS & PARABLES: God's Wisdom for Living, 16 studies by Dee Brestin. *694-6*

ECCLESIASTES: God's Wisdom for Evangelism, 13 studies by Dee Brestin. *212-6*

AMOS: Israel on Trial, 13 studies by Whitney Kuniholm. *043-3*

JONAH, HABAKKUK, & MALACHI: Living Responsibly, 12 studies by Margaret Fromer & Sharrel Keyes. *432-3*

THE GOD WHO UNDERSTANDS ME: The Sermon on the Mount, 15 studies by Gladys Hunt. *316-5*

MARK: God in Action, 18 studies by Chuck & Winnie Christensen. *309-2*

LUKE: Following Jesus, 20 studies by Sharrel Keyes. *511-7*

JOHN: Eyewitness, 24 studies by Gladys Hunt. *245-2*

ACTS 1-12: God Moves in the Early Church, 15 studies by Chuck & Winnie Christensen. *007-7*

ACTS 13-28: God Moves in a Pagan World, 14 studies by Chuck & Winnie Christensen. *008-5*

ROMANS: Made Righteous by Faith, 14 studies by Gladys Hunt. *733-0*

1 CORINTHIANS: Problems & Solutions in a Growing Church, 16 studies by Charles & Anne Hummel. *137-5*

EPHESIANS: Living in God's Household, 13 studies by Robert Baylis. *223-1*

PHILIPPIANS: God's Guide to Joy, 8 studies by Ron Klug. *680-6*

COLOSSIANS: Focus on Christ, 9 studies by Luci Shaw. *132-4*

LETTERS TO THE THESSALONIANS, 8 studies by Margaret Fromer & Sharrel Keyes. *489-7*

LETTERS TO TIMOTHY: Discipleship in Action, 13 studies by Margaret Fromer & Sharrel Keyes. *490-0*

HEBREWS: From Shadows to Reality, 13 studies by Gladys Hunt. *338-6*

JAMES: Faith in Action, 10 studies by Chuck & Winnie Christensen. *421-8*

HOW SHOULD A CHRISTIAN LIVE?: 1, 2, & 3 John, 13 studies by Dee Brestin. *351-3*

REVELATION: The Lamb Who Is the Lion, 13 studies by Gladys Hunt. *486-2*

BUILDING YOUR HOUSE ON THE LORD: Marriage & Parenthood, 16 studies by Steve & Dee Brestin. *099-9*

THE CHURCH: Pictures of Christ's Body, 12 studies by Lee Eclov. *155-3*

DISCIPLESHIP, 12 studies by James & Martha Reapsome. *175-8*

EXAMINING THE CLAIMS OF JESUS, 7 studies by Dee Brestin. *246-0*

GUIDANCE & GOD'S WILL, 12 studies by Tom & Joan Stark. *324-6*

HIGHER GROUND: For the Believer Who Seeks Joy and Victory, 14 studies by Steve & Dee Brestin. *345-9*

LET'S PRAY TOGETHER, 8 studies by Margaret Fromer & Sharrel Keyes. *801-9*

RELATIONSHIPS, 15 studies by Gladys Hunt. *721-7*

WOMEN WHO ACHIEVED FOR GOD, 14 studies by Winnie Christensen. *937-6*

WOMEN WHO BELIEVED GOD, 13 studies by Winnie Christensen. *936-8*